VICTO
THE WIDOWED QUEEN

THE COLOURFUL PERSONAL LIFE OF
QUEEN VICTORIA – PART 3

ILLUSTRATED WITH PORTRAITS FROM THE
AUTHOR'S COLLECTION

Susan Symons

SUSAN SYMONS
FASCINATING ROYAL HISTORY

Published by Roseland Books
The Old Rectory, St Just-in-Roseland, Truro, Cornwall, TR2 5JD

Copyright ©2017 Susan Symons

ISBN 13: 978-0-9928014-7-2
ISBN 10: 0992801478

For Mimi – the best aunt in the world.

CONTENTS

1

INTRODUCTION

The marriage of Queen Victoria and Prince Albert is one of the most famous relationships in history. But Albert died in middle age and Victoria spent twice as much of her life as his widow than as his wife. This book is about Victoria's thirty-nine years of widowhood after Albert's early death, when she became the doyenne (longest serving) of European sovereigns and the matriarch of a huge clan.

Widowhood did not bring out the best in Victoria's character. From babyhood she was used to being the centre of attention in the family and the focus for an entourage of courtiers in her household. While Albert was alive, he kept the worst of her qualities in check, but after his death she put her own needs first and became self-centred, obstinate, and dictatorial. The widowed queen demanded total devotion from her household and expected to control the marriages of her younger daughters so as to keep them at her beck and call. But Victoria's better qualities could also inspire love and affection in those around her, particularly in her later years. She was essentially soft-hearted and loyal, a good friend to have in time of trouble, and always saw her entourage, including servants, as individuals.

The first years of her widowhood were the least successful years of Victoria's reign. The widowed queen immured herself in extreme grief and refused to carry out the ceremonial duties of a monarch. As a result her popularity with the public suffered and there were calls for her to abdicate. She survived this dip and, in the years that followed, gradually got over Albert's death and emerged from self-imposed gloom. But her seclusion in her private homes, far from London, fuelled scandalous rumours about her private life.

1. Victoria as a new widow in a mournful portrait next to Albert's bust.

The story of Victoria's widowhood includes the men in her life. At only forty-two when Albert died, the widowed queen was still a desirable catch but she never considered another foray into the royal marriage market. Victoria enshrined Albert's memory and remained his grieving widow for the rest of her life. But in widowhood she still needed male company and support. She formed a close relationship with a male servant, flirted with her prime minister, and became very fond of a handsome son-in-law. Towards the end of her life she had a puzzling relationship with a much younger man.

Albert's death left Victoria as the mother of nine fatherless children, aged between four and twenty-one. As a widow, her family grew to huge proportions, with forty grandchildren and thirty-eight great-grandchildren when she died. Many of their stories are almost as fascinating as Victoria's own. Her children and grandchildren married across the thrones of Europe and by the time of her death most European monarchs were related to the widowed queen. History has labelled Victoria as *The Widow of Windsor*, for her display of permanent grief, but also as *The Grandmamma of Europe*, for the inter-related network of European royalty that descended from her. Through her daughters

2. Victoria gazes devotedly at Albert in this life-sized statue of the couple in period costume.

and granddaughters, she passed on the awful disease of haemophilia, for which there was then no cure, bringing tragedy to their families and contributing to the collapse of thrones.

During her married life, Victoria came to depend on Albert for everything and was not used to taking any action or making any decision without his advice. On his death she was rudderless and had to learn how to stand on her own two feet. In widowhood she grew into a figure of considerable authority, insisting on her rights and demanding deference – from her family and household, her ministers, and from fellow monarchs. They were all in awe of her. Even the *Iron Chancellor* of Prussia, Prince Otto Bismarck, came out from his meeting with the widowed queen mopping his brow! As a female monarch in an age before female emancipation, Victoria was in a most unusual position for her time, and she needed to be tough to maintain her authority.

By the end of her reign, Victoria was an institution and the icon of the age. After more than sixty-three years, there were few people

who could remember a time when she had not been on the throne. She was the symbol of Britain's superpower status and the monarch of two hundred million subjects in an empire that stretched around the globe. Queen Victoria is a British monarch in history whose name everyone knows.

This is the third of my books about *The Colourful Personal Life of Queen Victoria*. The idea for these books started when my mother asked me to give a talk about my longstanding interest in Queen Victoria to her women's group and to show them some of my collection of portraits. The first book, called

3. Victoria in her widow's cap after a quarter of a century as a widow.

Young Victoria, is the story of the early years of her life, including the difficult childhood that formed her resolute character and how she came to the throne aged only eighteen. *Victoria & Albert*, the second book, looks at her marriage to Albert and how she balanced the very different roles of sovereign and Victorian wife and mother. This third book, *Victoria, The Widowed Queen*, covers the long years of her life alone after Albert's early death.

Victoria's forty-year correspondence with her eldest daughter Vicky

Queen Victoria was a prolific letter writer and some of her thousands of letters have been published. These are a marvellous source for historians. Most notable is the voluminous correspondence with her eldest daughter Victoria (Vicky), who became kaiserin (empress) of Germany. For more than forty years, between Vicky's marriage in February 1858 and her mother's death in January 1901, the two women wrote to each other twice a week, exchanging family news and gossip and discussing state affairs. We are fortunate that these fascinating and often indiscreet letters survive, since both sides of the correspondence had a lucky escape!

When Victoria died, Vicky was also terminally ill with cancer. Her letters to her mother would normally have been in England, but Vicky had temporarily borrowed these back and had them in her home at Schloss Friedrichshof in Germany. Now Vicky wanted to keep her letters out of the hands of her son, Kaiser Wilhelm II, whom they portrayed in an unfavourable light. When the new king, Edward VII, came to visit his dying sister, Vicky used the opportunity to ask his secretary, Frederick Ponsonby, secretly to smuggle her side of the correspondence back to England.

Ponsonby's later publication of the letters caused controversy, with arguments about what Vicky had intended when she entrusted them to her brother's secretary and whether Ponsonby should have published. But, whatever his motives, publishing the letters helped to show Vicky's side of the story of her poor relationship with her son.

At the end of the World War II Friedrichshof was requisitioned by the American army and used as an officers' club. During these years the schloss suffered much damage and pilfering. Such was the concern that George VI sent the royal librarian and his assistant to Friedrichshof to locate the other side of the precious correspondence (Victoria's letters to her daughter) and bring these to England. The assistant in question was Anthony Blunt, who later rose to become keeper of the king's pictures; even later he was revealed as having been a Soviet spy since his Cambridge days in the 1930s —the fourth man to Burgess, Maclean, and Philby!

My books are a personal view of Queen Victoria's life story, from many years of researching and reading about her. They are not intended as a comprehensive account of her reign and times, but instead focus on her as a woman. Victoria lived in a time when kings and queens

4. Four generations of British monarchs photographed in 1894.

played a greater role in state affairs than they do today and she and her family undoubtedly had an impact on the history of Europe. The poor relationship between her son, King Edward VII, and her grandson, German Kaiser (emperor) Wilhelm II, was a factor contributing to the rift between Britain and Germany that led to World War I.

Victoria the Widowed Queen is illustrated with portraits and other memorabilia of the queen and her family from my personal collection. There are charts and family trees at the back of the book to help the reader get to grips with her large family and these are referred to at appropriate points in the text. A timeline provides an overview of key dates. As in the first two books, I have used some of Victoria's own words to help tell her story. The queen was a prodigious letter writer and also kept a daily journal all her life, from the age of thirteen. Although these sources have been edited prior to publication, they still provide a fascinating record and Victoria's own voice from history comes down to us loud and clear.

More than a century after her death, Victoria's life story still has the power to entrance us. More books have been written about Queen

Victoria than any other British monarch from history and almost every year there is a new biography exploring a different aspect of her life. Two highly successful films starring Dame Judi Dench portray Victoria's life in widowhood – *Mrs Brown* (about her relationship with her highland servant, John Brown) and *Victoria & Abdul* (about her fondness for her Indian secretary, Abdul Karim). For me Queen Victoria is as fascinating today as many years ago, when I found that portrait of her in the attic which sparked off my interest in her story and was the beginning of my collection.

5. Victoria in the last year of her life.

The British succession from Queen Victoria to the present day

Queen Victoria *was determined that all future kings of Great Britain would be called Albert after her beloved husband. She wanted their eldest son Bertie to reign as King Albert I, his son as King Albert II, and so on. But, so far, there has not been any king of Great Britain called Albert.*

*Bertie was christened Albert Edward – Albert after his father and Edward after his grandfather (Victoria's father, Edward, Duke of Kent). But when Bertie succeeded his mother in 1901, he deliberately rejected his father's name and chose to reign under his second name as **King Edward VII**.*

*The next heir was Bertie's eldest son. In deference to Victoria wishes, he was christened Albert Victor after both his grandparents (Albert after Albert and Victor as the male form of Victoria). However his parents much preferred the name Edward (another of his Christian names), and he was always known as Eddy in the family. Eddy died before his father, so it was Bertie's second son, George, who succeeded him as **George V**.*

*The eldest son of George V was christened Edward Albert (Edward after Eddy and Albert on Victoria's insistence). But his parents also preferred another of his names and he was known as David. He reigned briefly under his first name as **Edward VIII** until he abdicated to marry Mrs Simpson. The next king was his younger brother, the second son of George V. His name was Albert but he chose to reign as **George VI** in tribute to his father!*

*George VI was succeeded by his eldest daughter **Elizabeth II**. The queen has three generations of heirs-in-waiting but none of them have the name of Albert. If they choose to reign under their own first names, Elizabeth II will be succeeded in turn by **Charles III**, **William V** and **George VII**. So it looks unlikely that Victoria's wishes will ever be fulfilled.*

Please see chart 1 for the succession to the British throne from Queen Victoria to Queen Elizabeth II and her heirs.

2

HOW AM I ALIVE...?

Prince Albert died at Windsor Castle near London on Saturday 14 December 1861 at ten forty-five pm. He died in the Blue Room, that Victoria later turned into a shrine. In Victorian times most people died at home (rather than in hospital or a hospice) and being at the deathbed was an important part of the grieving process. So the Blue Room was crowded with the royal family and courtiers, waiting to witness Albert's last moments.

Soon after midnight the bell of St Paul's Cathedral called *Great Tom*, rung only for the death of the monarch or a national calamity, began to toll. Next morning church bells were tolling all over the country and this is how most of Victoria's subjects found out the terrible news.

It was ten years before Victoria could bring herself to write down the events of Albert's last day. Since childhood, the queen had followed the unalterable habit of keeping a daily journal. But the events of Saturday 14 December 1861 were so traumatic that there is no entry in her journal for this day, or the two weeks that follow. And it was not until February 1872 that she was at last able put down on paper ('with the help of notes scrawled down at the time') what happened on the day of Albert's death. This is how she described the end.

Two or three long but perfectly gentle breaths were drawn, the hand clasping mine, & (oh! It turns me sick to write it) *all all* was over...I stood up, kissing his dear heavenly forehead & called out in a bitter agonising cry: 'Oh! My dear Darling!' & then dropped on my knees in mute, distracted despair, unable to utter a word or shed a tear![1]

Women did not go to funerals and the chief mourners at Albert's on 23 December were two of his sons – twenty-year-old Bertie, the prince of Wales, and his eleven-year-old brother, Arthur. (See chart 2 for Victoria's nine children with their ages when their father died.) Victoria was hustled away from Windsor to Osborne House on the Isle of Wight before the funeral took place. This was a sensible precaution given the doctors believed an outbreak of typhoid at the castle had caused

6. Albert's mausoleum at Frogmore; Victoria chose the site within days of his death and often visited during her widowhood.

her husband's death. But she found it hard to leave the place where they had last been together and, when the moment came, was almost hysterical with sobbing and had to be cajoled into the waiting carriage. She was overwhelmed by the catastrophe that had torn her life apart and could not comprehend how she could go on living without Albert.

How am I alive after witnessing what I have done? Oh! I who prayed daily that we might die together and I never survive him! I who felt, when in those blessed arms clasped and held tight in the sacred hours at night, when the world seemed only to be ourselves, that nothing could part us. ... I never dreamt of the physical possibility of such a calamity – [2]

Victoria clung desperately to any memory of her dead husband. Before his body was put in the coffin, she commissioned sketches and photographs of the corpse, a death mask of his face and a cast of his dead hands. She slept with Albert's night-shirt in her arms and the cast of his hands within easy reach. For the rest of her life, wherever she slept, a coloured photograph of her dead husband hung above the pillow on his side of the bed. Preserving mementoes of the dead was not uncommon in the Victorian age, but the widowed queen took it to extremes. She kept Albert's rooms exactly as he left them ... and as if he were about to return. Servants laid out fresh clothes every day, brought hot water for shaving, and scoured his chamber-pot.

7. Statue of Albert at Balmoral.

11

Albert's last illness

The royal family were staying at Windsor Castle when Victoria's journal for 28 November 1861 records that her husband had caught a chill. After years of overwork and fragile health, Albert was already exhausted and depressed. The stress of dealing with Victoria's emotions in the last few months had been intolerable, and now Albert was also distraught from finding out about his eldest son's affair with an actress. The prince went rapidly downhill, becoming weak, feverish, and confused, so that by 7 December Victoria wrote in her journal 'I seem to be living in a dreadful dream'[3].

At the start of his last illness Albert was very restless, wandering from room to room. But eventually he decided to settle in the room of Windsor Castle called the Blue Room. His choice of sickroom was portentous as the Blue Room was where Victoria's two predecessors, King William IV and King George IV, had both died. The royal doctors diagnosed Albert's illness as typhoid, contracted from poor sanitation and contaminated drinking water at Windsor Castle. But they played down the severity of his condition because they were concerned about his wife's fragile mental state. As a result Victoria was unprepared and in denial right up to Albert's last day. Her prime minister (Lord Palmerston) was much more concerned. He urged that more doctors be consulted, but the queen indignantly pushed him away.

In the late afternoon of 14 December it was clear the end was near. Albert's bed was moved into the centre of the room to make space for family and courtiers to cluster round him. In the room, as well as his wife and elder children, were the four doctors treating the prince, his devoted valet, plus other family and courtiers. Only his beloved eldest daughter Vicky (his favourite child) was absent. She was pregnant with her third child in Prussia and forbidden by her doctors to travel.

More recently the cause of death as typhoid has been challenged. There were no other reported cases at the castle as might have been expected if the drains were defective. Also, Albert had been unwell for some considerable time and his symptoms went back years. It seems more likely he suffered from a longstanding complaint, possibly stomach cancer, or Crohn's disease.

From the first days of her widowhood, Victoria began to plan grand public memorials to preserve the memory of her beloved husband. Before she was finished, there were Albert statues all over the country – how he would have hated that! Victoria did her husband a disservice in the way she sanitised and whitewashed his memory, so that he has come down in history as a worthy but dull character. The first official biography of the prince was published only five years after his death and portrayed Albert as without fault. Ostensibly the author was Albert's secretary (Charles Grey); in reality it was ghost-written by Victoria. I like to think the real man was more interesting than she wanted us to believe!

8. As a widow Victoria spent as little time as possible at Buckingham Palace.

At Osborne House the new widow whirled in a vortex of grief and despair. Victoria had suffered a nervous breakdown earlier in the year, following the death of her mother, the duchess of Kent. Her grief for her husband was now so intense that the royal doctors feared for her sanity. Albert had controlled every aspect of his wife's life and Victoria vowed passionately to continue to carry out his wishes. Ten days after Albert's death she wrote to her uncle (King Leopold of Belgium) that '... *his* views about *every* thing are to be *my law*! And *no human power* will make me swerve from *what* he decided and wished – '[4]. This would become a mantra she used to justify her obstinacy.

In the seclusion of Osborne, Victoria buried herself in gloom. For weeks she took all her meals in her room, shut off even from the royal household. When ministers came from London, she didn't want to see them and suggested they communicate indirectly, using her daughter Alice as a go-between. And she refused to attend a meeting of the Privy Council (a very important duty for the monarch), eventually and very reluctantly agreeing to an awkward compromise. Victoria sat in one room, with the Privy Council in another and the door between the two rooms ajar. The privy councillors could not see the queen, but she could hear what was said. It was a sign of worse to come.

9. In this photo with Bertie and his new bride on their wedding day, Victoria defies the joy of the occasion and gazes grimly at Albert's bust.

3

WHERE IS BRITANNIA?

The months and years passed but still Victoria could not be coaxed out of seclusion, to show herself in public, or to carry out the ceremonial duties of a monarch. She did not want to get over Albert's death or to move on in her life. She was consumed by guilt over her failure to recognise the seriousness of his illness, and any lessening of grief would have seemed like a betrayal. When Albert was alive he urged his self-centred wife not to focus just on her own emotions; without him she could only wallow in her feelings. She spent much of her time in her remote homes at Osborne House on the Isle of Wight and Balmoral Castle in Scotland, and as little time as possible at Buckingham Palace in London. When her eldest son Bertie, heir to the British throne, was married in March 1863, the wedding was not in Westminster Abbey or St Paul's Cathedral, so that the public could see the show, but in the small chapel at Windsor Castle, with Victoria shrouded from view. And even in the wedding photos, the image of dead Albert took centre stage (see illustration 9).

Victoria said she was determined to do her duty as queen, but she took the view that the hours spent at her desk each day (dealing with the red boxes of official paperwork) should be enough; more she could not do. She had a horror of being put on public display, and gawped at in her misery by the curious. The widowed queen compared the ordeal of opening parliament to an execution and said she would not wish it on her bitterest enemy. When asked to carry out this ceremonial function in 1866 (nearly five years after Albert's death), she wrote to her Prime Minister, now Lord John Russell (using the third person) –

> The Queen *must say* that she does feel *very bitterly* the want of feeling of those who *ask* the Queen to go to open Parliament ... why this wish should be of so *unreasonable* and unfeeling a nature, as to *long to witness* the spectacle of a poor, broken-hearted widow, nervous and shrinking, dragged in *deep mourning,* ALONE *in* STATE as a *Show,* ...[5]

Victoria would not grasp that the most important function of a monarch is to be seen, in order to retain the loyalty and affection of

10. Bertie, the affable prince of Wales, and his beautiful young Danish wife Alexandra (Alix); they were very popular and perversely Victoria was jealous.

their subjects. When she was pressed to make a public appearance she resorted to the equivalent of a royal sick-note, and got her doctor to say that her health would not stand it. Some historians have suggested that the widowed queen used her health as an excuse and that she was quite capable of appearing in public when it suited her convenience. For example, she did in the end open parliament in 1866 (for the first time since Albert's death) probably because she wanted the session to vote a dowry to her daughter

11. Alix with her first child, Albert Victor.

(Helena) and an allowance to her son (Alfred). But even then she was extremely difficult over the arrangements, refusing to wear her robes of state or read out her speech, and sitting stony-faced throughout.

But I don't think we should doubt that Victoria came close to a total breakdown after Albert's death. She suffered from deep depression and her legs would hardly carry her. The widowed queen genuinely believed she must have peace and quiet to maintain her mental equilibrium. When a guest at Windsor Castle started to discuss politics in June 1862, she stopped him quickly, tapping her forehead and calling out 'My reason, my reason.'[6].

At first there was a swell of public sympathy for the queen in her great loss. Albert's death came as a complete shock because the official bulletins on his illness (issued by the royal doctors) were so bland that nobody had understood the prince was mortally ill. The whole country went into mourning and shops selling mourning clothes and black material ran out of stock. Extra seamstresses had to be employed to meet demand. Christmas 1861 was the gloomiest that anyone could remember.

17

But there was also an expectation that in due course Victoria would emerge from retirement, as did other widows, and resume her role as queen. Etiquette demanded that a widow keep full mourning (wearing only black) for a year and a day, followed by a further six months of half-mourning (when she was permitted to wear white, grey or lilac). But two years went by, then three, and still Victoria remained invisible. The public functions of the monarchy were carried out by her eldest son Bertie, the affable prince of Wales, and his beautiful young wife, Alix (Alexandra). They were very popular and perversely, although she did not want to do these duties herself, Victoria was jealous. But they were not accepted as a substitute for the queen.

12. Bertie with his two sons, Albert Victor (Eddy) and George (Georgie), at the time they became naval cadets.

Queen Victoria and food

After Albert's death, Victoria turned to food for comfort and she put on weight. Photos of her before he died show that, despite nine pregnancies, she was still relatively svelte. But in the decades after 1861, her portraits chart her increasing size. The Fashion Museum in Bath has one of the widowed queen's dresses from 1899 and this has a forty-five inch (one hundred and fourteen centimetres) waist.

Even as a young woman, Victoria liked her food and had a tendency to overeat. She was only around five feet tall (one and a half metres) and her journal for 13 December 1838 (when she was nineteen) records that 'to my horror' she weighed eight stone thirteen pounds (fifty-seven kilos)! Lord Melbourne (Victoria's first prime minister) recommended exercise and suggested that she should only eat when she was hungry. Victoria's response was that she would be eating all day since she was always hungry!

The meals served to the widowed queen were elaborate and extensive. But she gobbled down her food and meals of several courses (aside from state dinners) were timed for half an hour. Victoria was always served first and as soon as she had finished, everyone's plates were taken away. If a courtier was a slow eater, they could go hungry! Victoria continued to overeat into old age and as a result was a martyr to indigestion. Only at the end of her life did her appetite fail and then she lost weight. The last time that she mentioned food with any pleasure in her journal was a month before she died.

So, rumblings began that the queen was shirking her royal duty. One cartoon showed an empty throne under the title *Where is Britannia?* A piece of graffiti appeared outside Buckingham Palace, with the words 'These commanding premises to be let or sold, in consequence of the late occupant's declining business.' In an anonymous pamphlet called *What does she do with it?*, the author (a member of parliament called George Trevelyan) calculated that, as Victoria did not come to London or entertain on a grand scale as her predecessors had done, she must be squirreling away most of the civil list voted to her by parliament.

The institution of monarchy was deeply rooted in British society, but Victoria's popularity plummeted and the 1860s were the low point in her reign. There were calls for her to abdicate in favour of her son, and a republican movement to abolish the monarchy altogether gained ground. Her family and courtiers remonstrated with the queen in vain. Like most obstinate and self-centred people, opposition only made Victoria more determined. Eventually, her nine children took the unprecedented and foolhardy step of jointly writing their mother a letter, urging her to come out of seclusion and save the monarchy. It is lucky this letter was overtaken by events and never sent; such impertinence would surely have met a volcanic response! What did save the monarchy and restore Victoria's popularity was the serious illness of the prince of Wales, during which he almost died.

13. Victoria and Bertie in the carriage procession to St Paul's for the Thanksgiving Service for his recovery from typhoid.

In December 1871 Bertie fell ill with typhoid – the same illness it was believed had killed his father ten years earlier. Bertie caught it at a shooting party in a country house where the sanitation was defective. Several other guests were also taken ill, and one died. As Bertie's fever rose, Victoria sat in her son's sickroom in his home at Sandringham House in Norfolk, listening to his delirious ravings. The house was packed with waiting relatives and courtiers and as the tenth anniversary of Albert's death approached, Bertie's life hung in the balance. Everyone worried history could repeat itself. But 14 December

14. Victoria in 1875 – she was gradually recovering from Albert's death.

came and the crisis passed. Bertie wasn't out of the woods yet, but he would get better. Unlike his father (who Victoria is alleged to have said died from 'want of pluck'), Bertie fought for his life – and won.

The illness and recovery of the prince of Wales gripped the nation and rejuvenated affection for the royal family. For once, Victoria found herself unable to resist a great public occasion and on 27 February 1872 mother and son rode together through the streets of London in an open carriage to a National Service of Thanksgiving in St Paul's Cathedral. Every inch of the route was lined with hundreds of thousands of happy and cheering spectators. Bertie was still pale and lame and his eyes filled with tears as he constantly raised his hat to acknowledge the cheers. At Temple Bar, in an act of pure showmanship, Victoria was seen to raise her son's hand and kiss it – the crowd went wild.

From then on, Victoria was secure in the public affection. She didn't make any great changes in her routine and she still rarely came to London. But she was gradually recovering from Albert's death and the grounded and confidant woman who looks out of the portrait of 1875 (illustration 14) is very different to that pathetic widow of ten years before (illustration 1).

Victoria's relationship with her eldest son also improved. After her husband died she could hardly bear to see Bertie, whom she blamed for his father's death. Albert's last illness took a sharp turn for the worst when he found out that his teenage son had lost his virginity to an actress. After his recovery, Bertie pledged to be a different man, but his mother continued to deny him any useful occupation and he returned to a pointless round of pleasure. Victoria's attitude towards him had softened and from now she better appreciated her son's good qualities.

15. Victoria liked fresh air and hated hot rooms or closed windows – here she takes afternoon tea out-of-doors, sitting in her carriage.

The Royal Household

The widowed queen sat at the centre of a large organisation devoted to looking after her. This was structured in layers, according to social class, with the queen at the pinnacle. Beneath Victoria and her family were the aristocratic courtiers who made up the Royal Household, then came professional attendants at her court (such as doctors, secretaries and governesses), and finally an army of servants (themselves organised into senior servants and the rest).

In 1895 an article in Strand Magazine listed twenty-four lady courtiers in the Royal Household, including the Mistress of the Robes (the most senior and always a duchess), ladies-in-waiting (the wives or widows of peers), women of the bedchamber (usually the daughters of aristocrats) and maids-of-honour (selected by the queen from good families). These lady courtiers were matched on the gentlemen's side by the Master of the Household, lords-in-waiting, grooms-in-waiting, and equerries. Not all the courtiers would be at court at the same time. They worked on a rota basis with, for example, one lady-in-waiting and two maids-of-honour living with Victoria (or being 'in-waiting') at once. Being in-waiting could be monotonous and there was a lot of hanging about. When she was appointed, one maid-of-honour was told by her mother 'You must accustom yourself to sit or stand for hours without any amusement save the resources of your own thoughts'⁸.

Below the aristocrats were the tutors, governesses, librarians, and other professionals who came from the middle classes. Their position could be awkward since they were not servants, but nor were they courtiers. When Dr James Reid was appointed as resident medical attendant in 1881, his written terms of engagement stated that he was not an official member of the Royal Household and would not therefore dine with them in the evening. The doctor took dinner in his room until the widowed queen heard he was hosting dinner parties there. She promptly changed the rules and from then on Reid ate with the household.

Reid also broke another of the widowed queen's rules by marrying one of her maids-of-honour. Victoria hated any of her courtiers getting married because she wanted their complete loyalty to be entirely to her. In 1863 she bewailed to her uncle (King Leopold of Belgium) that a favourite lady-in-waiting '... has, most unnecessarily, decided to marry!! ... I thought she would never leave me!'

Victoria was a stickler to work for and there were many petty rules and regulations. She was quick to spot transgressions but disliked confrontation and often communicated in writing or through intermediaries. There were compensations, including the excellent food and (particularly after the grim years of the 1860s) plenty of entertainment. Although the widowed queen rarely went out in public, there were private performances in her homes of opera, plays, concerts, Gilbert and Sullivan, and even dances. Another favoured entertainment was **tableaux vivants**, *when the royal family and courtiers dressed-up to pose in famous scenes from history.* **Fotheringay** *at Osborne in January 1890 depicted Victoria's ancestor, Mary Queen of Scots, saying goodbye to her ladies before her execution. The Scottish queen was played by the widowed queen's fourth daughter, Louise.*

4

MRS BROWN

In December 1864 a Scottish servant travelled south to Osborne House on the Isle of Wight, where Victoria was in residence. John Brown was a ghillie (or gamekeeper) on the Balmoral estate and the idea to bring him to Osborne originated with the queen's doctor. It was hoped that having a reliable and trusted servant to lead her pony might encourage Victoria to ride more and take her out of herself. The plan was a success and John Brown was soon promoted to be *The Queen's Highland Servant*, attending her indoors as well as out. But their close relationship caused tension and jealousy in the queen's family and household, and led to scandalous rumours, persisting until this day, that they were lovers – even that Victoria married him and became Mrs Brown.

John Brown was a burly and rugged highlander. He was born into a family of poor crofters (smallholder farmers) at Craithie, near Balmoral, in 1826. Brown was seven years younger than Victoria and thirty-eight years old when he came to Osborne. He was already known to the queen as he had been employed at Balmoral since she and Albert acquired the estate. Victoria had a great admiration for the common people of the Scottish highlands, and for her John Brown embodied

16. John Brown was a burly highlander.

their best qualities. He was down to earth, forthright, honest, and loyal. Brown was not a courtier and he never prevaricated or tried to flatter the queen. He treated Victoria as he would any woman, from whatever class, and always told her exactly what he thought. Victoria could be obstinate and opinionated, and she hated being crossed, but she did not mind Brown's straight-talking because she knew it was from the best of motives and that he was devoted to her welfare.

Victoria always had a deep-seated need for a strong male figure in her life and, after Albert's death, she longed still to come first with someone. Soon after Brown took up his new duties, she wrote to Vicky

I feel I have here and always in the house a good devoted soul ... whose only object and interest is my service, and God knows how I want so much to be taken care of.[10]

Her Highland Servant was always there attending to her comfort – part bodyguard, part ladies' maid, part errand boy. Brown kept people away when she didn't want to see them and wherever Victoria went, he was close by. He rescued her from a carriage accident at Balmoral; lifted her in and out of her wheel chair when she was so ill in 1871 that she could not walk; and got between her and a would-be assassin when a young Irish Nationalist called Arthur O'Connor waved a pistol in her face outside Buckingham Palace in 1872. Brown looked after the widowed queen until he died and in all his eighteen years of service, he never took a single day's holiday. He was rewarded for his loyalty with salary rises, medals, and generous gifts, and also with Victoria's friendship. He never took advantage, or betrayed her. His only vice was that he drank to excess and became a chronic alcoholic, suffering delirium tremens. Victoria chose to overlook that he was frequently what was called 'bashful' or 'confused' – euphemisms for drunk!

But, for Victoria's entourage, what at first had seemed a good idea to help the queen over her grief, quickly turned sour. Brown's privileged access to the queen was seen as usurping their rights, and what's more he was a commoner and a servant! Brown's brusque manners and lack of deference were infuriating for courtiers who felt themselves his social superiors. Victoria herself was surprisingly free from class or race prejudice, but the enclosed, hot-house world of the royal household ran on such distinctions. Tensions ran high and Brown was at the centre of frequent rows over what were essentially trivial matters.

17. Balmoral Castle in the Scottish highlands.

Balmoral Castle

In 1868 Victoria published a book called '**Leaves from the Journal of Our Life in the Highlands**'. This was a compilation of extracts from her journal about the royal family's holidays at Balmoral Castle, the highland home built by Albert. The book was dedicated to the memory of her husband 'who made the life of the writer bright and happy' but John Brown features heavily in the contents. 'Leaves from the Journal' portrays a mundane round of picnics, outings, and other leisure pursuits. But to a public starved of any sight or sound of their queen, the book was riveting. It became an instant best-seller, and outsold even 'The Moonstone' by Wilkie Collins (the first-ever detective novel) that was published the same year!

Victoria and Albert visited Scotland for the first time in 1842. Albert immediately loved the highlands which reminded him of the Thuringian hills of his home in Germany. They decided on a highland home and first leased and then bought (in 1852) the Balmoral Estate. The old castle was too small, so Albert built a distinctive new castle next to it in Scottish Baronial style, and then knocked down the original. The new Balmoral was decorated in peculiarly highland style with oceans of tartan and armies of stags' antlers. The royal couple threw themselves with gusto into their highland holidays with deer-stalking, trekking expeditions, picnics, bonfires, and highland dancing! These happy times were recorded in Victoria's journal.

After Albert died, Victoria spent more time at Balmoral, staying here for several months in the autumn. Like Osborne House (built by Albert in the 1840s), the castle was her refuge, far away from London and the prying public gaze, where she could nurse her grief in seclusion. But her love of Balmoral was not shared by the Royal Household who (behind the queen's back) complained about the lack of comforts and pure boredom of weeks in a remote location, with very little to do. The six hundred miles journey from London was also a major inconvenience for her government.

Balmoral was purchased privately by Victoria and Albert and it remains in the ownership of the sovereign. Like her great-great-grandmother, Queen Elizabeth II holidays at the castle for several weeks every autumn.

What became called *The Great Pony Row* erupted at Balmoral when the gentlemen of the household were banned from taking out ponies without express permission, while Brown apparently had free run of the stables. There was another row when the queen instructed that the Smoking Room must be closed at an early hour so that Brown could get off to bed. This was the only place where the men were allowed to smoke (Victoria abhorred the habit) and they were affronted that a servant's comfort should take priority over theirs.

Victoria always took Brown's side and dismissed all the rumblings about him as

> ... *ill-natured* gossip in the higher classes, caused by dissatisfaction at *not forcing* the Queen *out* ... [of her seclusion][11]

She was not ashamed of her friendship and saw no reason to hide it. She commissioned the portrait in illustration 18 by Sir Edwin Landseer and this was exhibited at the Royal Academy in 1867, where it attracted the most unfavourable attention. Victoria is shown seated on her

18. Landseer's 1867 portrait of the queen with John Brown drew unwelcome attention to her Highland Servant.

horse outside Osborne House. She is working on official business, and discarded papers and the red box litter the ground. Two of Victoria's daughters (Helena and Louise) are sitting nearby and John Brown, wearing his highland regalia, holds the horse's head.

It is a most unlikely scenario and it draws attention to John Brown. If Victoria had appeared more often in public, or John Brown hadn't been so noticeable because of his kilt, then probably he would have been accepted as just another servant. But as it was, rumours circulated about what went on in the queen's seclusion. Some people said Victoria had gone mad and John Brown was her keeper; others that he was a spiritualist medium who put her in touch with Albert. But the most persistent rumour was that Brown was her lover. Jokes circulated referring to Victoria as *Mrs Brown* and the magazine *Punch* published a spoof version of the *Court Circular* (the official court calendar) in which John Brown is treated as a member of the royal family. An article in a Swiss newspaper alleged that Victoria couldn't appear in public because she was pregnant by her Highland Servant.

19. John Brown in attendance (left, wearing a kilt)
as Victoria presents a military medal.

John Brown died at Windsor Castle on 27 March 1883. The cause of death was erysipelas (a recurring skin infection), aggravated by alcoholism. Victoria felt his loss deeply and wrote to Brown's family that ' ... we all have lost the best, the truest heart that ever beat'[12]. She put up a life-sized statue of her friend in highland dress at Balmoral, with the inscription below by the poet Lord Alfred Tennyson.

> Friend more than servant, Loyal, Truthful, Brave
> Self less than Duty, even to the Grave.

As soon as he came to the throne, Bertie had this statue moved out of sight.

After the death of John Brown, courtiers quietly disposed of his diaries; and after the death of Victoria, her daughter doctored hers, editing out references to John Brown. I believe this censorship was counterproductive and that, if we could read the originals, we would see the relationship between Queen Victoria and John Brown for what it was – an unusual friendship, crossing gender and class, between a lonely woman and her devoted servant. Destroying the evidence has not erased John Brown from the record as intended, but only fuelled speculation as to what secrets that evidence contained.

20. Victoria in a photo of 1866.

The queen's dressers

Among the ranks of servants in Victoria's employ were her dressers and wardrobe maids. These were important and senior positions and the posts were normally filled by recommendation from within the royal network. The uncle of Marianne Skerrett, who joined as dresser in 1837 and stayed for twenty-five years, had been in royal service before her. Because of the intimate and confidential nature of their job, some of these women became as close to Victoria as any of her family or courtiers.

The roles of dresser and wardrobe maid were similar, but dresser was the more senior position. The duties of these jobs were demanding and Victoria was an exacting mistress. When a brooch was lost, she blamed the wardrobe maid, alleging it could not have been pinned on properly.

Her dressers and wardrobe maids were responsible for the queen's appearance, personal care, and grooming, as well as her extensive wardrobe and jewellery. They had to combine the skills of ladies maid, hairdresser, beautician, milliner, and dressmaker. Victoria changed several times a day and everything she took off had to be checked over for mending or cleaning, sent to the laundry, ironed, and put away. The dressers and wardrobe maids made many items of the queen's clothing by hand and dealt with tradesman for the rest. When Victoria travelled, they went with or ahead of her, selecting, packing, unpacking, and caring for everything she would need. Those on duty started work in time to get Victoria up in the morning and were not finished until after she had gone to bed. One was even required to sleep on a sofa in the room next door in case the queen wanted anything in the night!

The long hours and relentless pressure affected the health of some – Frieda Arnold left after less than five years for medical reasons. But others stayed with the widowed queen for decades. Emilie Dittweiler (who was Frieda's replacement) was dresser for thirty-three years, and Annie Macdonald wardrobe maid for forty-one.

5

THE FAERY QUEEN

During the years of her friendship with John Brown, Victoria's other close male relationship was with Benjamin Disraeli, who was her prime minister twice in the 1860s and 1870s. This was also an unlikely pairing as Disraeli did not have the wealthy aristocratic background of most senior politicians at that time. He was middle-class, a converted Jew, wore his hair in long ringlets, and wrote romantic novels. He could only afford to be in politics because he married the widow of his financial backer. Mary Anne was garrulous, over-dressed and just as odd as her husband. She is supposed to have once told the queen that she slept with her arms around Disraeli's neck! Mary Anne was twelve years older than Disraeli but the marriage worked and one of Mary Anne's sayings was

Dizzy married me for my money. But, if he had the chance again, he would marry me for love[13].

As prime minister, Disraeli set out to charm the queen. Everyone likes flattery, he said, and when it comes to royalty, you should lay it on with a trowel. He attributed his success to treating Victoria as a woman, whereas his political opponent, William Gladstone, Disraeli said, treated her as a public department. Gladstone was prime minister four times and Victoria came to loathe him.

21. Victoria with Disraeli when she visited his home at Hughenden Manor.

Disraeli was attracted to older women and took delight in serving a middle-aged female monarch. At his first audience as prime minister, he took the queen's hand and murmured, 'In loving loyalty and faith'. He wrote to her in the flowery language of a novelist, so that Victoria said she never had such letters before. Disraeli called Victoria *The Faery Queen* after *Titania* in *A Midsummer's Night Dream* and when she sent him boxes of primroses from Osborne House, said they were a sign that 'your Majesty's sceptre has touched the enchanted isle'. He was always careful to give the impression that he valued the queen's experience and was seeking her advice. But away from the palace he explained his strategy for dealing with Victoria as 'I never refuse, I never contradict, I sometimes forget'.

When Disraeli's first ministry fell, the queen acceded to his request and made Mary Anne a peeress in her own right. Victoria had initially considered Disraeli's wife to be vulgar, but came to appreciate their devotion as a couple. During his second spell in government (after Mary Anne had died) Victoria created Disraeli Earl of Beaconsfield and granted him a signal honour by visiting his home at Hughenden Manor in 1877 (see illustration 21). This was a public display of friendship she did not show to any other of her prime ministers except for the first, Lord Melbourne, when she went to Brocket Hall in 1841. The queen had ten different prime ministers during her long reign.

22. This colourful portrait commemorates Bertie's tour of India in 1876.

Disraeli knew just how to bring drama and theatre into the routine of state business. When Britain bought a large shareholding in the Suez Canal during his second spell as prime minister, Disraeli personalised it for the queen, sending her the message 'It is just settled. You have it Ma'am'! In 1876 he gave Victoria the title she craved, when he pushed the bill through parliament that made her Empress of India. The timing coincided with Bertie's successful tour of the sub-continent and was proclaimed at a magnificent durbar (gathering of Indian princes) at Delhi in 1877.

Victoria had long been fascinated by India and would have liked to go there herself, but she also wanted to be an empress to get parity with the emperors of Austria, Germany and Russia. She regarded herself as the senior European sovereign and did not take kindly to any emperor trying to claim rank on the grounds she was only a queen. Her eldest daughter would become empress of Germany and it was unthinkable that Vicky should outrank her!

From now Victoria signed as *VRI* – Victoria, Regina et Imperatrix (Queen and Empress).

6

ONE OF MY DAUGHTERS
TO BE ALWAYS IN ENGLAND

After Albert's death, Victoria soon came to feel that she needed the devotion of a daughter living with her. Victoria and Albert had five daughters, aged between twenty-one and four when their father died. (Chart 2 shows all Victoria's children with their ages at Albert's death; chart 3 gives details of their marriages and the numbers of their own children.)

In the early months of Victoria's widowhood, the role of supportive daughter was admirably carried out by her second daughter, eighteen-year-old Alice. A great burden fell on Alice's shoulders when Albert became ill. Vicky was already married and living in Prussia, so that Alice was the eldest daughter at home. There were no professional nurses at this time, and sick people were looked after at home by their female relatives. Alice helped to nurse her dying father and then took on the main role of comforting her bereaved mother. Many years later, Alice still remembered those terrible first nights, when she lay next to her sobbing mother until they fell asleep from exhaustion in the early hours of the morning.

But Alice was already engaged – to a German prince called Louis of Hesse-Darmstadt. Louis feared his fiancé would back out of their engagement, but the marriage went ahead. It had been arranged by Albert before he died and Albert's widow was determined to carry out his wishes. Alice's wedding took place six months after her father's death in the strict privacy of the dining room at Osborne House and was described by her mother as 'more a funeral than a wedding'[14]. The bride was permitted a white wedding dress but otherwise Victoria insisted on a black trousseau.

23. Victoria's second daughter, Alice, in a portrait before her father died.

Victoria saw no reason why the marriage should interfere with her own needs and the first years of Alice's married life were blighted by her mother's constant demands for lengthy visits back to Britain. Her first child was born at Windsor Castle during such a long stay, nine months after the wedding, on 5 April 1863. But Louis and Alice had responsibilities as the future rulers of the German principality of Hesse-Darmstadt. And, besides, these visits to Britain were very expensive and (for royalty) they were not particularly well off. When Alice failed to comply with her mother's wishes, she sadly fell out of favour.

Alice inherited the haemophilia gene from Victoria and her younger son died at two years old, from internal bleeding following a fall. She also passed on the gene to two of her daughters, who took it into the Prussian and Russian royal families. Alice was the first of Victoria's children to die aged thirty-five, from diphtheria. By a horrible coincidence she died on 14 December 1878, the same day of the year as her father seventeen years before. She left behind five motherless children under sixteen.

The next daughter was Helena, aged fifteen when Albert died. Most of Victoria's clan had nick-names in the family and Helena's was Lenchen. When it came to Lenchen, Victoria was determined that there should be no grand marriage to the heir to a German throne, as had been arranged by Albert for the two eldest girls. This daughter must marry a prince without a patrimony, and he must agree to live in England so that Lenchen could remain on call to act as her mother's secretary. She wrote to Vicky that

> ... Lenchen could not and would not leave me, as in my terrible position I required one of my daughters to be always in England[15].

24. Victoria's third and fourth daughters –
Helena (Lenchen) on the right and Louise on the left.

Victoria's choice fell on an impoverished prince called Christian of Schleswig-Holstein, a younger son without any inheritance. He was fifteen years older than his fiancé, going bald, and rather dull. Some of her brothers and sisters protested (much to Victoria's annoyance), but Lenchen was compliant and they married in 1866. The marriage aggravated an already deep divide among Victoria's children caused by the wars between Prussia and Denmark over the German duchies of Schleswig-Holstein. Not only was Vicky married to the king of Prussia's son, and Bertie to the king of Denmark's daughter, but now Lenchen married the brother of the third claimant to these territories (the duke of Schleswig-Holstein)! No wonder that Victoria had to ban any discussion of the issue on family occasions!

Lenchen's marriage was a success and the couple had five children, including a son who died as a small baby. This is why there is a question mark over whether Lenchen was a carrier of haemophilia. She spent a good deal of her time with her mother, as Victoria had intended, but always had her own, separate, home.

25. Victoria with *Baby* (her youngest daughter Beatrice) and their dogs.

The marriage of the fourth daughter, Louise, who was thirteen when Albert died, also caused controversy in the family. Louise was the most beautiful of Victoria's daughters and the most unconventional. She was artistically talented, attended lessons at Art School, and became a notable sculptress. Louise broke with royal convention when she took a husband from outside the tight circle of European royalty. She married a wealthy British aristocrat – Lord Lorne (who later succeeded his father as duke of Argyll). Victoria supported bringing new blood into the family and wrote to Bertie, when he objected to his sister's fiancé, saying that times had changed and marriages with small German princes ('German beggars as they most insultingly were called … ') were looked on with dislike[16].

But Louise's marriage does not seem to have been much of a success. The couple spent most of their time apart and had no children, so that we cannot know whether Louise was a carrier of haemophilia. There are all sorts of rumours about them – that Lorne may have been homosexual, and that Louise had affairs, including with a brother-in-law. She seems to have been a lively and indiscreet character who was prone to create trouble in the royal household and did not always get on with her sisters!

When Louise married in 1871, this left just one unmarried daughter still at home. Beatrice was the youngest of the five, and only four years old when Albert died. *Baby* (as she was called by Victoria throughout her childhood) was one of the few people who were able to lighten her widowed mother's gloom. But growing up at Victoria's side had an effect on the little girl's personality and a cheeky toddler became a shy and reserved adult. She seemed to accept her destiny as her mother's companion; but just to be on the safe side, Victoria banned any talk of young men or marriage in front of Beatrice. Then, at a family wedding in 1884, Beatrice met a German prince called Heinrich (Henry) of Battenberg. Henry was not out of the top drawer of royalty, since his father had married below his rank, but he was handsome and dashing and Beatrice fell in love.

When Beatrice said she wanted to get married, Victoria was appalled and selfishly refused to countenance the match. For months she wouldn't speak to her daughter and they communicated by notes

26. Caricature of Beatrice at the time of her marriage.

pushed across the breakfast table. But Beatrice stuck to her guns and, faced with an impasse, Victoria eventually gave way and compromised. Henry resigned his commission in the Prussian army and the queen agreed to the marriage provided the couple lived with her and Beatrice carried on as her companion and secretary. The wedding took place on 23 July 1885 in the small village church at Whippingham, near Osborne House on the Isle of Wight. Beatrice wore Victoria's wedding veil and was walked up the aisle by her mother and her eldest brother, Bertie (both behind her in illustration 27).

Victoria lost the fight to prevent this daughter marrying but the wedding heralded some of the happiest years of her life. She enjoyed having a handsome young man about the house again, and became very fond of this son-in-law. Henry was a well-liked and genial figure who brought more gaiety into the royal household and was well able to manage his mother-in-law. Victoria also found joy in her four Battenberg grandchildren (three boys and a girl) born between 1886 and 1891, who lived with her.

But after ten years of married life Henry longed for wider horizons. He felt stifled by his life at court and wanted to serve his adopted country. He persuaded Victoria to let him take part in a military expedition to the Ashanti region of West Africa (now part of Ghana), departing in

December 1895. But he caught malaria as soon as he arrived and died on 20 January 1896, on board the ship back to England. Victoria had foreseen this possibility and given instructions that, should Henry die, his body must be brought home for burial. This presented a huge challenge to the crew of HMS Blonde when Henry died at sea in the tropics where bodies have to be dealt with quickly. But they were up to it – they made a waterproof coffin out of old biscuit tins, and filled it with rum to act as a preservative! Henry is buried in the church at Whippingham, where he had been married.

Beatrice went away for a month to mourn her husband. Then she and her mother went on as before, for the rest of Victoria's life. Beatrice is a known carrier of haemophilia and two of her four children inherited the disease. Her middle son was a sufferer and died following a medical operation on his knee, and her only daughter was a carrier who took it into the royal family of Spain.

27. Beatrice married Henry of Battenberg in the village church at Whippingham on the Isle of Wight on 23 July 1885.

The Battenberg/Mountbatten family

Beatrice's new husband was one of the four sons of Prince Alexander of Hesse-Darmstadt. Because their father had married below his station, his sons were not entitled to his rank but instead were given the subsidiary title of princes of Battenberg. These four boys had interesting lives and the eldest, called Ludwig or Louis, was the grandfather of Philip, Duke of Edinburgh.

Although a German prince, Louis chose to follow a career in the British navy. He joined the senior service at fourteen and rose to become First Sea Lord of the Admiralty (head of the British navy). In 1884 he married Victoria of Hesse-Darmstadt who was the granddaughter of the widowed queen (the daughter of Alice). But Louis's German birth and connections made him suspect on the outbreak of World War I in 1914 and he was forced to resign. And in 1917, amid anti-German public feeling and hysteria, he was requested by George V to drop his German titles and anglicise his German family name. Battenberg was turned into Mountbatten by reversing the two halves of the name and translating 'berg' into 'Mount' (or mountain).

Louis and Victoria had two sons and two daughters. Their elder daughter, called Alice, married Prince Andreas of Greece and Denmark and they were the parents of Prince Philip, Duke of Edinburgh. Philip was a prince of Greece and Denmark but when he became a naturalised British subject prior to his marriage to Princess Elizabeth in 1947, he changed his surname to Mountbatten. This raised the question whether the name of the British royal family would in future be Mountbatten, but this has remained as Windsor.

Louis and Victoria's younger daughter became queen of Sweden. Their younger son was Lord Louis Mountbatten (Earl Mountbatten of Burma) who was murdered on a holiday fishing trip in 1979, with other members of his family, when their boat was blown up by the IRA (Irish Republican Army).

7

GRANDMAMMA OF EUROPE

In 1887 Victoria celebrated her Golden Jubilee – fifty years on the British throne. In the jubilee portrait in illustration 30 she is still wearing her widow's weeds, but heavy black crepe has now given way to luxurious satin and silk and is trimmed with expensive lace and sparkling jewels.

A galaxy of royalty crowded into London to celebrate the Jubilee and take part in a glittering procession from Buckingham Palace to Westminster Abbey. Victoria took the opportunity of having so many of her family around her to commission the magnificent group portrait (by the Danish artist Laurits Tuxen) shown in illustration 28. Fifty-four of her family members, across three generations, are included in this magnificent picture. The poor artist got on the wrong side of family politics when trying to put the composition of his picure together – the Danish-born princess of Wales refused to be shown next to the crown prince of Prussia, remembering the wars between their countries over Schleswig-Holstein twenty years before, and Victoria's son Arthur didn't want to be near her newest son-in-law, presumably on the grounds that, as a mere Battenberg, Henry was only a second-rate royal!

28. Victoria commissioned this group portrait
of fifty-four of her family members.

The focal point of the picture is Victoria as the matriarch. This is the woman who, as a new bride, said she did not want to have a big family. Her family had grown to colossal proportions. As well as nine children, there would be forty grandchildren (three of them still to be born at the time of the 1887 jubilee) and thirty-eight great-grandchildren before she died. (Chart 4 shows the numbers of Victoria's descendants born year by year.) Many years before, Victoria had written wearily in a family letter

> … I fear the seventh grand-daughter and fourteenth grand-child becomes a very uninteresting thing – for it seems to me to go on like the rabbits in Windsor Park![17]

But she did take an interest in them all and expected to have a say in their upbringing. She was a better grandmother then she had been a mother. Victoria kept in touch with her extended family, sending letters of advice, arranging marriages, and generally exerting her authority.

They were all in awe of her – even her eldest grandchild, Wilhelm (Willie) of Prussia (Vicky's first child, born in 1859). He would become Kaiser Bill (Wilhelm II) and was, as much as anyone, responsible for starting World War I.

The young man leaning against the fireplace on the right of the group portrait is Victoria's most important grandchild – this is Prince Albert Victor (Eddy), who was Bertie's eldest son and the next heir after him to the British throne. But Eddy died of pneumonia in 1892, aged twenty-eight, and never became king. History has given him a poor reputation, suggesting that Eddy was a dull-witted child who became a degenerate young man. There are stories that he frequented male brothels, and he has even been named (wrongly) as a suspect for Jack the Ripper! The message is that it could have been a good thing Eddy died to make space for his honest and upright younger brother Georgie, later King George V. Georgie even acquired his elder brother's fiancé! At the time of his death Eddy had recently become engaged to Princess May (Mary) of Teck. Victoria considered her to be

29. A caricature portrait of Eddy.

eminently suitable as a future queen consort of Great Britain and, in due course, May dutifully switched her affections, married the younger brother, and became Queen Mary.

So many of Victoria's family have fascinating, and sometimes tragic, personal stories. Five of her granddaughters became queens (of Greece, Norway, Romania, Russia and Spain). One of the figures in the background of the jubilee family portrait is Victoria's granddaughter

Alix of Hesse-Darmstadt (Alice's daughter), the doomed future tsarina of Russia. Alix was never a popular figure in Russia and was called *the funeral bride* because she married Tsar Nicholas II (Nicky) only a month after his father's death. Hundreds were trampled to death during the celebrations for their coronation. Alix inherited the defective gene from Victoria, and the haemophilia of her only son, Alexis, was a factor in the fall of the Romanov dynasty and the Russian revolution. Alix and her entire family (husband, son, and four daughters) were murdered by the Bolsheviks in 1918.

Victoria's lost grandsons

In 1877 Victoria commissioned a touching statue for the private chapel at Windsor Castle, showing an angel cradling small children in her arms. This was to commemorate the five of her grandsons who had died young. Infant mortality was a significant risk and more than a third of Victoria's grandsons died as babies or boys. It is hard to imagine the grief and distress their loss must have caused.

The first to go was little Sigismund (Sigi) of Prussia, Vicky's third son, who died of meningitis in 1866, aged twenty-one months. Alice's two-year-old son Friedrich Wilhelm (Frittie) was the first victim of haemophilia in his generation. In 1873 he accidentally tumbled out of an open window during a game with his older brother and by evening the toddler was dead from an internal haemorrhage. Bertie lost his youngest son, John, at one day old in 1871; and Lenchen suffered the loss of two baby boys – Harald at eight days in 1876, and a still-born son the following year. Two more little boys died after the statue was finished. Vicky's youngest son Waldemar (Waldie) died from diphtheria in 1879, aged eleven; and a son was stillborn to Affie's wife later that same year (Affie was Victoria's second son Alfred).

In all, ten of Victoria's grandsons died during her widowhood and chart 5 shows a complete list. Her granddaughters proved more robust and only one died as a child. Four-year-old Marie (May) fell victim to the same diphtheria epidemic that killed her mother Alice in December, 1878.

At the time of the golden jubilee, Beatrice was expecting her second child. Ena (Victoria Eugenie of Battenberg) also made a great marriage – to King Alfonso XIII of Spain. But her wedding dress was splattered with blood when a terrorist threw a bomb on her wedding day. Ena was also a carrier of haemophilia and two of her four sons had the disease; a third was disabled. Alfonso and Ena lost their throne when Spain became a republic in 1931.

Victoria became a great-grandmother in 1879 (just before her sixtieth birthday) when Vicky's eldest daughter, Charlotte of Saxe-Meiningen, gave birth to her only child. Little Feodora

30. Queen Victoria at the time of her Golden Jubilee.

(Feo) was a difficult child who never got on with her mother and spent much of her childhood with her grandmother (she is shown leaning against Vicky in the left foreground of the Tuxen picture). Historians now believe that both Charlotte and Feo suffered from porphyria, a gene disorder which affects the chemical make-up of the body and can produce both physical and mental symptoms. This disease was also hereditary in the British royal family – the most famous sufferer being Victoria's grandfather, King George III.

In 1894, the succession to the British throne was secured to the fourth generation. The photo on page 6 shows four generations of British monarchs – Victoria with her son Bertie, prince of Wales (later Edward VII), his son Georgie, duke of York (George V), and his son David (Edward VIII and after his abdication, duke of Windsor).

49

The group portrait of Victoria's family was painted one hundred and thirty years ago. But it includes a link to more recent times. The little girl on the far right of the picture is Alice of Battenberg, who will be the mother of Prince Philip, Duke of Edinburgh.

Vicky and Fritz

To my eye, the dominant figure in the Golden Jubilee group portrait, after Victoria herself, is the tall man standing on the right, wearing a white military uniform. This is Victoria's best-loved son-in-law, Crown Prince Friedrich (Fritz) of Prussia, the husband of Vicky. When Albert picked Fritz as a husband for Vicky, he envisaged them uniting Germany under a constitutional Prussian monarchy. But these dreams had come to nothing. Thirty years later, Fritz was still waiting to come to the throne and had been side-lined by Bismarck in favour of his eldest son, Willie. Fritz even had to insist on his right to come to London and take part in the jubilee procession.

And now Fritz was a dying man. Some months before the jubilee a growth appeared in his throat and the German doctors diagnosed cancer of the larynx. Vicky fought against her husband's diagnosis, initially keeping it secret from Fritz and favouring the side of an English doctor who said the growth was benign. She was a spiky character who had never fitted in in Prussia; and her high-handed behaviour now made her even more unpopular. The English doctor was wrong and it was cancer. Fritz lived long enough to succeed his father as kaiser (emperor) of Germany but died, aged fifty-six, on 15 June 1888 after a reign of just ninety-nine days. He was too ill to make any of the changes he had planned and had to accept the hated Bismarck as his prime minister.

Vicky did not have a good relationship with her son Willie, who became Kaiser Wilhelm II. He treated his widowed mother shabbily, refusing her the use of palaces she wanted and virtually accusing his parents of treason. Vicky used her own money to build a new palace, far away from Berlin, and dedicated it to Fritz in memory of their happy marriage. She died there, from cancer, six months after her mother.

8

THE MUNSHI

In 1887, in honour of the Golden Jubilee, two Indian attendants were sent from India to join the widowed queen's entourage. A carefully selected group of Indian princes had been invited to the jubilee and it was hoped to create a good impression if the queen had some Indian staff to wait at table. Victoria was deeply interested in India and excited by the novelty of these exotic new servants. One of the newcomers was a tall, slender, and good-looking twenty-four-year-old young man, called Abdul Karim. He soon made his mark with the queen and was relieved of all servants' duties and promoted to be her Indian Secretary, with the title of *Munshi* (meaning teacher).

I have never been able to make up my mind about the Munshi. To Victoria he was the voice of India. He gave her lessons in Hindustani (Urdu) and cooked her curries (which she liked). But to her long-suffering entourage he was anathema; it must have seemed that no sooner had the problem of John Brown gone away (with his death in March 1883), than this even more troubling relationship with a servant began.

Courtiers did everything they could to discredit the Munshi – alleging he had lied about his background and family's social class, in order to convince Victoria he was above domestic service; that he

31. The queen's preferential treatment of her Munshi (Abdul Karim) caused resentment and tension in the royal household.

had links to a radical group in India and could be leaking government information about India that came his way; and that he was implicated in the theft of one of her brooches. Even the other servants made complaints about him. It did not help that the Munshi obtained special privileges from the queen that were not afforded to her courtiers – such as exclusive use of a carriage on the royal train during her travels, when everyone else was squashed up. He was very prickly about his status and position in her household, complaining to the widowed queen whenever he felt slighted or treated as a servant. Victoria always believed the Munshi's side of the story and said she found her Indian

Secretary invaluable. She treated Abdul Karim as an indulgent mother might treat her son; loading him with gifts and honours and taking visiting royalty to his home to meet his wife. His relationship with the queen made Abdul Karim a rich and respected man in India. When he went home to India on leave, Victoria missed him and looked forward to his return.

What I can't decide is whether her courtiers were right and the Munshi was a slippery customer who exploited his relationship with Victoria, or whether they were just airing their prejudice because they didn't want to associate with an Indian servant. Probably it was a bit of both.

So there were frequent rows about the Munshi, which often left Victoria upset, shaken, and in tears. Some of the worst of the rows were when she insisted he be included in her annual holiday to the south of France (in the 1890s Victoria went to the French Riviera each spring). The gentlemen of the household threatened to resign en masse, rather than have to treat him as an equal and eat at the same table. But Victoria would not give in. The Munshi stayed put and he was still in the queen's service when she died, living in the three homes she provided for him, at Balmoral, Osborne and Windsor.

32. Victoria on a morning outing during her spring holiday at Cimiez near Nice in 1897.

The Coburg succession

In 1893 Duke Ernst II of Saxe-Coburg and Gotha died. Because he was childless, the succession to his duchy (Coburg) fell to the sons of his younger brother, Albert. It would prove a poisoned chalice that uprooted two of Victoria's English grandsons and forced them to become German. (Please see chart 6 for the succession to Coburg.)

The succession fell first on Victoria's second son Affie – Alfred, Duke of Edinburgh. Affie joined the Royal Navy at fourteen, retiring as Admiral of the Fleet. Awkward questions were raised about whether a German duke should sit in the House of Lords, and in Germany over on which side a retired British admiral would be in event of war! Affie became more difficult, drank too much, and died from throat cancer in 1900. His only son (also called Alfred and known as Young Affie), had died the year before him – aged twenty-four.

Young Affie was sent to Germany as a child and only saw his parents occasionally. Perhaps this made him rootless and was a factor when he went off the rails as a young officer in the Prussian army. Affie caught syphilis, neglected his duties, and was forced to leave his regiment in disgrace. He died in mysterious circumstances during the celebrations for his parents' twenty-fifth wedding anniversary. Syphilis was a shameful disease and his death was hushed up, allowing rumours to circulate. One story is that he tried to shoot himself but it is more likely he died from his disease.

Young Affie's death reopened the problem of an heir to Coburg. Next in line was Victoria's third son, Arthur, Duke of Connaught, but he renounced the succession for himself and his son. And so the choice fell on sixteen-year-old Charles Edward (Charlie) of Albany, the posthumous son of Leopold (Victoria's haemophiliac youngest son). Charlie was taken away from Eton and sent to Germany, and his name germanised to Karl Eduard. As a British prince succeeding to a German throne, poor Charlie was in a cleft stick. He was stripped of his British titles during World War I, while in Germany his English origins made him suspect. Perhaps he over-compensated by trying to be 'more German than the Germans'? Charlie is a dark spot in the family history. In the 1930s he joined the Nazi party and became a follower of Hitler.

Why did Victoria stick to the Munshi? Some people said she was afraid of him and that he shouted at her in private. This has the hallmark of an unscrupulous younger man preying on a vulnerable old woman – except that Victoria was the queen and could easily have had him dismissed at any time. There is no doubt that Victoria was very attached to Abdul Karim and her last prime minister (Lord Salisbury) thought she actually enjoyed all the emotional upset. Perhaps it was reminiscent of those delicious rows with Albert, so many years before!

33. Victoria with the Russian tsar and tsarina (her granddaughter Alix) during their state visit to Balmoral in 1896; they were recorded by the newly invented cine camera (the first time royalty appeared on film).

After the widowed queen's death, Beatrice and Alix turned up at the Munshi's home and demanded the return of Victoria's letters to him. They burned them in a bonfire outside the house. The new king (Bertie) wanted to destroy any record of his mother's relationship with Abdul Karim. The Munshi's grace-and-favour homes were reallocated to courtiers and he and Victoria's other Indian attendants were dismissed and sent back to India. The Munshi lived quietly in India for the rest of his life in the grand home he built on land given him by Victoria. He suffered ill health and died only eight years after his patroness, aged forty-six. His family were Muslim and his relatives lost everything when they were forced to flee to Pakistan on the partition of India in 1947. But miraculously, a few mementoes survived of the glory days when Abdul Karim was Victoria's favourite and mixed with European royalty. Their rediscovery helped to bring his story back to life in the film *Victoria & Abdul* starring Judi Dench.

9

SO WEAK AND UNWELL

By the time of her Diamond Jubilee in 1897, Victoria was becoming frail. The Thanksgiving Service for her sixty years on the throne had to be held outside St Paul's, because the seventy-eight-year-old queen suffered so badly from rheumatism she could no longer manage the steps into the cathedral. She remained sitting in her carriage during the service, with the clergy and choir ranged on the steps beside her.

The widowed queen had cataracts and her eyesight was going, making it increasingly difficult to read or write. Victoria found this a 'terrible privation'. She complained about her spectacles and harangued her private secretary to write larger, and to use darker ink, so that she could see what he had written. But soon she had to rely on her daughters or ladies-in-waiting to read papers to her and dictate the answers.

Many of those she loved had died before her. When Victoria made her last will she hoped

... to be reunited to my beloved Husband, my dearest Mother, my loved Children [Alice and Leopold were dead] and 3 dear sons-in-law [Fritz of Prussia, Louis of Hesse-Darmstadt, and Henry of Battenberg]

... Also I hope to meet those who have so faithfully & so devotedly served me especially good John Brown and good Annie Macdonald ... [her wardrobe maid for more than forty years][18].

34. In her Diamond Jubilee portrait, Victoria wears a bracelet with a miniature of Albert; her brooch is the family order of Victoria and Albert, which she instituted soon after he died.

For the last few years of her life Victoria's health was in decline. Photos such as illustration 35 show a tired old lady. The widowed queen made a state visit to Ireland in April 1900 but after that she did not venture away from her three homes (Balmoral, Osborne and Windsor). She had no appetite now and was losing weight; she couldn't sleep properly at night and then slept on into the day, much to her annoyance.

She was lame following a fall, could only walk with difficulty using a stick, and had to use her 'rolling chair' (wheelchair). Her memory was letting let her down. She was weak and apathetic. There was bad news from Africa, where a favourite grandchild, Christian Victor (Christle) of Schleswig-Holstein, died of fever serving in the Boer War; and more bad news from Germany, where two more of her children were terminally ill from cancer. Affie died in July 1900 and Vicky would only survive her mother by a few months.

But Victoria kept to her routine and on 18 December 1900 she moved homes for the last time, to celebrate Christmas at Osborne House. Another blow fell on Christmas Day when the lady-in-waiting on duty, and Victoria's friend of fifty years, was found dead in her bed. Lady Jane Churchill had joined the royal household in 1854. When Victoria dictated her journal on New Year's Day 1901, she wrote

> Another year begun, - I am feeling so weak & unwell, that I enter upon it sadly[19].

The last entry in Queen Victoria's journal, begun all those years before when Victoria was thirteen, was for 13 January 1901.

35. This photo of Victoria in 1899 shows a tired old lady.

By now her doctor was very worried about the queen. Sir James Reid had been part of the royal household for twenty years, travelling everywhere with Victoria as part of her suite. In her final years, he was probably the most important man in her life. But the first time her doctor ever saw the widowed queen in bed was during these last weeks at Osborne. He wrote in his diary for 16 January 1901:

> The queen had rather a disturbed night, but was very drowsy … , and disinclined to get up, although she kept saying in a semi-confused way that she must get up. I saw her asleep in bed in the forenoon, as I was rather anxious about her, and the maids said she was too drowsy to notice me. This was the first time I had ever seen the queen when she was in bed. She was lying on her right side huddled up and I was struck by how small she appeared[20].

36. Victoria during her state visit to Ireland in April 1900.

Reid was struggling to get Victoria's children to understand that their mother's life was coming to an end. So now the doctor took the bold step of overriding Beatrice's instructions and suggesting to Bertie he cancel his weekend at Sandringham and come to Osborne instead. The doctor also secretly sent a telegram to Victoria's grandson – Kaiser

Wilhelm II. Willie was much disliked by his English relatives because of his arrogant and pompous personality and his unkind treatment of his mother. The kaiser had a love-hate relationship with his mother's country (Britain), but he much admired his grandmother and had asked Sir James to keep him informed.

Willie was born with a damaged left arm (a legacy of his difficult breach birth) which never grew to full size and was useless. It is interesting to speculate how much this disability contributed to his unattractive personality, and how much he blamed his mother for it. As a child, Willie endured agonising and futile treatments to try to cure the arm, and as a grown-up he was at pains to disguise it. In portraits he is usually shown with his left hand in his pocket. But for once Willie behaved well when he arrived at Osborne. He came as a grandson rather than a sovereign and did not expect any special treatment. Before she died, Victoria was supported in bed in a semi-sitting position, by her doctor kneeling on one side and Willie on the other.

Queen Victoria died at 6.30pm on Tuesday, 22 January 1901. Her son-in-law, the duke of Argyll (Louise's husband) likened her last moments to those of a great ship going down. Her granddaughter-in-

37. Original cartoon called *The God of War* ridiculing Kaiser Bill (Willie) during World War I.

law (the future Queen Mary) spoke for many of Victoria's subjects when she wrote in her diary 'The thought of England without the Queen is dreadful even to think of. God help us all'[21].

Queen Victoria and dogs

Throughout her life, Queen Victoria was devoted to dogs. She acquired her first dog (a King Charles Cavalier Spaniel called Dash) as a thirteen-year-old and her journal records with delight how she threw a ball for the little dog and he bounded after it at full gallop. From then on she was never without her dogs as companions and when she lay dying at Osborne in January 1901, she asked for her little Pomeranian, called Turi, to be put on the bed.

Victoria's dogs are often mentioned in her journal and they appear regularly in her portraits and photographs. Illustration 25 shows Victoria and her daughter Beatrice at Osborne in 1875 with four of their dogs. Number 38 shows her with Sharp the Collie. When Sharp died in 1879 Victoria wrote in her journal she could not believe that the dear faithful dog was no more. He was buried at Windsor with a headstone reading 'Sharp, the favourite and faithful Collie of Queen Victoria from 1866 to 1879.'

Victoria helped to improve the welfare of dogs and other animals. From early in her reign she was the patron of the Royal Society for the Prevention of Cruelty to Animals (RSPCA), granting the society royal status in 1840 with the right to use the prefix 'Royal'. The queen refused to follow canine fashion and none of her dogs had their tails docked or their ears clipped and no puppies were disposed of as unwanted. In 1885 Victoria became the patron of the Battersea Dog's Home, which has remained under royal patronage ever since. She was also an early supporter of Crufts, exhibiting six Pomeranians at the first show in 1891 – called Fluffy, Nino, Mino, Beppo, Gilda, and Lulu. They all won prizes!

Victoria passed on her love of dogs to her children, including her son Bertie who became Edward VII. He was the owner of a famous royal dog – Caesar the Fox Terrier. When the king died in 1910, Caesar was inconsolable and touched the hearts of the nation as he walked behind the coffin in the funeral procession. Caesar lies at the feet of his master's effigy on his tombstone, immortalised in white marble.

Up until the present day, dogs have continued to be important to members of the royal family.

Many years before, Victoria had written instructions regarding her death, saying that

> ... her faithful and devoted personal attendant (and true friend) Brown should be in the room and near at hand, and that he should watch over her earthly remains and place it in the coffin, ...[22]

But Brown was dead, so this last service was carried out by her doctor. In accordance with her wishes he carefully placed a number of items inside her coffin. There were mementoes of her beloved husband Albert and other members of her family. Placed in her left hand and concealed by flowers, was a photo of John Brown and a small case with a lock of his hair. Not even her close family knew that these were there.

38. The widowed Victoria with her dog Sharp.

39. This lavish illustration from her Diamond Jubilee year shows Victoria on the right with her three direct heirs, and portraits of the queen across her long reign on the left. Also shown bottom left are her eldest daughter Vicky, German Empress Friedrich III, and Vicky's son Willie, Kaiser Wilhelm II.

10

THE END OF AN ERA

For ten days Victoria's coffin rested in a temporary chapel in the dining room at Osborne, before the long journey to Windsor Castle for her funeral. From Cowes the coffin travelled across the Solent on the royal yacht *Alberta* to board the funeral train at Portsmouth. It was an extraordinary spectacle as the little *Alberta* steamed between a guard of honour of two long lines of warships (British and German) firing gun salutes; preceded by torpedo boat destroyers and followed by more royal yachts, including the German emperor's *Hohenzollern*.

At Windsor railway station, on the last part of the long journey, the coffin was transferred to a gun-carriage. But then there was a major mishap when one of the horses shied and snapped the traces (the straps attaching the carriage to the horse's harness). No-one was sure if the remaining horses could bear the load up the hill to the castle and the idea of the gun-carriage and coffin coming loose and careering backwards, mowing down the principal mourners including the new king and the kaiser, was too awful to think about! Then Prince Louis of Battenberg (the grandfather of the duke of Edinburgh) stepped forward to suggest that the gun-carriage be dragged by sailors and thus began a tradition that has been followed for later monarchs.

On 4 February Victoria's coffin was laid to rest next to that of Albert, in the opulent mausoleum she built for him at Frogmore, near Windsor Castle. She chose the site just days after his death, and often visited the mausoleum during her forty years as a widow. When Albert died, the widowed queen expected soon to follow him to the grave and commissioned marble coffin effigies (full-length reclining statues) of both of them for the mausoleum. She survived her husband for so long that no-one at first could remember where her effigy was stored. Although Victoria lived to be eight-one, her effigy in the mausoleum shows her frozen in time at forty-two, her age when Albert died.

After Victoria's death the world went on as before, but only for a while. The first years of the twentieth-century were a halcyon period for British high society, named *the Edwardian era* after the reign of her son Bertie, as King Edward VII. But the personal enmity between Bertie and his nephew Willie (Kaiser Wilhelm II) was one reason why their countries drifted apart. Britain drew closer to republican France, and Germany found herself allied to the decrepit Austro-Hungarian Empire. After the Austrian Archduke Franz Ferdinand was assassinated in June 1914, Europe exploded into war. Millions died, Victoria's family

40. King Edward VII and Queen Alexandra with Kaiser Wilhelm II and Kaiserin Auguste Viktoria.

was torn apart, and European thrones toppled. World War I was the great divide in our history and nothing was ever the same again. If Victoria could have lived (she would have been ninety-five in June 1914), she might never have allowed it to happen.

World War I and the thrones descended from Queen Victoria

Through their marriages, Victoria's children and grandchildren created a family network of related European monarchs. On the eve of World War I, her grandchildren sat on seven thrones – Britain, Germany, Greece, Norway, Romania, Russia, and Spain (see chart 7). But these relationships counted for little when the lines were drawn and cousins were on opposite sides of the devastating conflict.

In August 1914, George V found himself at war with his cousin Willie, the kaiser of Germany, but in alliance with Russia, where both the tsar and tsarina were also his cousins (Nicky on his mother's side and Alix on his father's). Other cousins were drawn in as the conflict took hold. In Romania, Queen Marie (a cousin George V had once hoped to marry, but she turned him down) eventually persuaded her husband, King Ferdinand, to side with the Allies (Britain, France, and Russia), and she became a national heroine as Romania was invaded by the enemy. In Greece, Queen Sophie did not fare so well and was tainted by her German birth (she was Willie's sister). Her husband, King Constantine I, tried to keep Greece out of the conflict and as a result was pushed aside by the Allies in 1917 in favour of his son. Of the seven countries whose monarchs were first cousins, only Norway (Queen Maud) and Spain (Queen Ena) were able to stay neutral in World War I.

By the end of the gruelling conflict, enough was enough and revolutions toppled the thrones of Russia (1917) and Germany (1918). George V kept his crown but only at the cost of disowning his cousins, the tsar and tsarina. The new government of Russia wanted to send the ex-tsar and his family into exile in Britain – George V, concerned about the shaky nature of his own position, turned this down. Nicky and Alix with their five children and loyal servants were murdered by the Bolsheviks in July 1918.

The throne of Spain survived World War I, but King Alfonso and Queen Ena went into exile in 1931. Their grandson, Juan Carlos was eventually restored in 1975; the current king of Spain, Felipe VI, is their great-grandson. The Greek monarchy staggered on until King Constantine I and Queen Sophie's grandson, King Constantine II, was deposed in 1973.

Since her death, Queen Victoria has achieved global superstar status. She succeeded to our throne at only eighteen and reigned for a total of sixty-three years, seven months, and two days. The widowed queen was hosting a visit from the tsar and tsarina of Russia at Balmoral when she overtook her grandfather, George III, as the longest reigning monarch in British history on 23 September 1896. Only Queen Elizabeth II has reigned for longer, overtaking Victoria on 9 September 2015.

And Victoria's story goes on today – her descendants still sit on the thrones of Great Britain, Norway, and Sweden. I think she would have been proud of her great-great-granddaughter, Elizabeth II. Victoria was also a great queen. Her personal achievement was to stabilise the British monarchy that, before her, was scandal-ridden and unpopular. And she gave her name to, and presided over, one of the most successful periods in British history – *the Victorian age.*

As I have tried to show in my books, Victoria was a real woman – passionate, loving, and loyal; but also obstinate, self-centred and controlling.

41. Victoria was a great queen.

LIST OF KEY DATES

1861. Prince Albert dies at Windsor Castle on 14 December.

1862. Victoria's second daughter, Alice, marries Louis of Hesse-Darmstadt.

1863. Marriage of Bertie, Prince of Wales to Princess Alexandra (Alix) of Denmark.

1864. John Brown relocates to Osborne, and will become Victoria's personal servant.

1866. Victoria reluctantly opens parliament for the first time since Albert's death.

Her daughter Helena marries Christian of Schleswig-Holstein.

Death of Sigismund of Prussia – the first of Victoria's grandchildren to die.

1867. Landseer's portrait of Victoria with John Brown is exhibited at the Royal Academy.

Publication of a cartoon called *Where is Britannia*, showing an empty throne.

1868. Disraeli is prime minister for the first time.

Later in the year he is succeeded by Gladstone (also prime minister for the first time).

1871. Marriage of Princess Louise to a British aristocrat.

Bertie falls desperately ill with typhoid fever.

1872. Thanksgiving service at St Paul's Cathedral for Bertie's recovery.

1874. Disraeli becomes prime minister for the second time.

1876. Victoria becomes Empress of India.

1878. Alice dies from diphtheria on the seventeenth anniversary of her father's death.

1879. Birth of Victoria's first great-grandchild – Feodora of Saxe-Meiningen.

1880. Disraeli retires as prime minister and dies the following year.

1883. Death of John Brown.

1884. Death of Victoria's haemophiliac youngest son, Leopold.

1885. Princess Beatrice marries Henry of Battenberg.

1887. Victoria's Golden Jubilee.

Abdul Karim (the Munshi) joins Victoria's staff from India.

1888. Vicky's husband succeeds his father as emperor of Germany, but dies only 99 days later from cancer.

1891. Birth of Victoria's fortieth and final grandchild.

1892. Death of Victoria's grandson, Albert Victor, the next heir after Bertie to the British throne.

1893. Victoria's second son, Alfred, becomes duke of Saxe-Coburg.

1894. Victoria's granddaughter Alix marries Tsar Nicholas II of Russia. The end of Gladstone's fourth and last stint as prime minister.

1896. Death of Victoria's son-in-law Henry of Battenberg.

Victoria overtakes her grandfather, George III, as the longest reigning British monarch.

1897. Victoria's Diamond Jubilee.

1900. Death of Duke Alfred of Saxe-Coburg.

1901. Victoria dies at Osborne House on 22 January.

Vicky dies in Germany on August 5.

CHARTS AND FAMILY TREES

1. The British succession from Queen Victoria to the present day

2. Victoria's nine children; with their dates of birth and ages when their father died

3. The marriages of Victoria's children

4. Victoria's grandchildren and great-grandchildren by the years of their birth

5. Victoria's grandsons who died young

6. The succession to Coburg

7. The thrones descended from Queen Victoria

1. THE BRITISH SUCCESSION FROM QUEEN VICTORIA

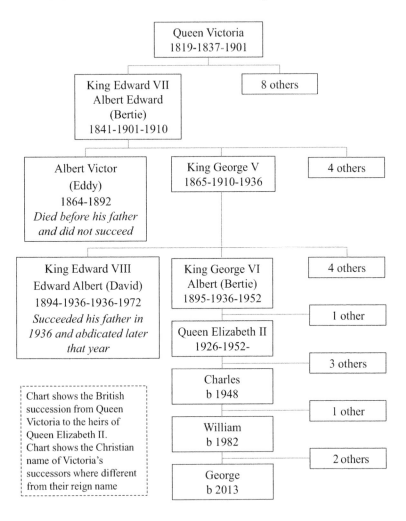

2. VICTORIA'S NINE CHILDREN
with their dates of birth and ages when their father died

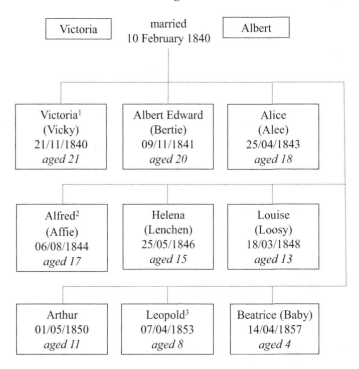

Three of the children were away from home when their father died. They were
1. Vicky, who was married and living in Prussia
2. Affie, who was in the navy
3. Leopold, who was spending the winter in the south of France for his health (he was a haemophiliac)

3. THE MARRIAGES OF VICTORIA'S CHILDREN

Vicky 1840-1901	m 1858	Prince Friedrich of Prussia (Fritz)	→	4 sons, 4 daughters
Bertie 1841-1910	m 1863	Princess Alexandra of Denmark (Alix)	→	3 sons 3 daughters
Alice 1843-1878	m 1862	Prince Ludwig of Hesse-Darmstadt (Louis)	→	2 sons 5 daughters
Affie 1844-1900	m 1874	Grand Duchess Marie Alexandrovna of Russia	→	*1 son 4 daughters
Lenchen 1846-1923	m 1866	Prince Christian of Schleswig-Holstein	→	*3 sons 2 daughters
Louise 1848-1939	m 1871	John Campbell Marquis of Lorne	→	No children
Arthur 1850-1942	m 1879	Princess Luise Margarete of Prussia	→	1 son 2 daughters
Leopold 1853-1884	m 1882	Princess Helene of Waldeck and Pyrmont	→	1 son 1 daughter
Beatrice 1857-1944	m 1885	Prince Heinrich of Battenberg (Henry)	→	3 sons 1 daughter

*Numbers do not include stillbirths

4. VICTORIA'S GRANDCHILDREN AND GREAT-GRANDCHILDREN BY THE YEARS OF THEIR BIRTH

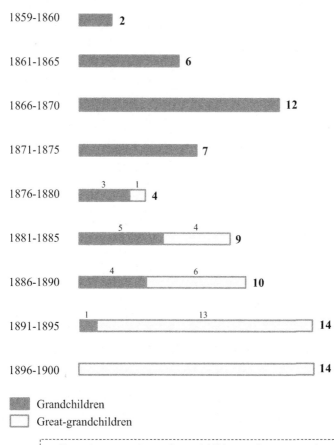

Grandchildren

Great-grandchildren

Chart shows numbers of grandchildren and great-grand-children born in each year band. Stillbirths are not included.

5. VICTORIA'S GRANDSONS WHO DIED YOUNG

June 1866
Sigismund (Sigi)
Vicky's third son,
21 months - meningitis

April 1871
Alexander John (John)
Bertie's youngest son
One day old

May 1873
Friedrich Wilhelm (Frittie)
Alice's youngest son
2 ½ years old - haemophilia

May 1876
Harald
Lenchen's third son
8 days old – haemophilia?

May 1877
Unnamed
Lenchen's youngest son
Stillborn

March 1879
Waldemar (Waldie)
Vicky's youngest son
11 years old - diptheria

October 1879
Unnamed
Affie's youngest son
Stillborn

January 1892
Albert Victor (Eddy)
Bertie's eldest son
28 years old - pneumonia

February 1899
Alfred (Affie)
Affie's eldest son
24 years – probably syphilis

October 1900
Christian Victor (Christle)
Lenchen's eldest son
33 years old – fever
in the Boer War

Chart shows the ten of Victoria's grandsons who died young during her lifetime.
One granddaughter (Marie, the youngest daughter of Alice) also died from diptheria in December 1878, at four-years-old.
Two further grandsons died prematurely after Victoria's own death. Beatrice's youngest son, Maurice, died of wounds in World War I in October 1914, aged 23; and her middle son, Leopold, died from haemophilia in April 1922, aged 33, following a knee operation.

---

6. THE SUCCESSION TO COBURG

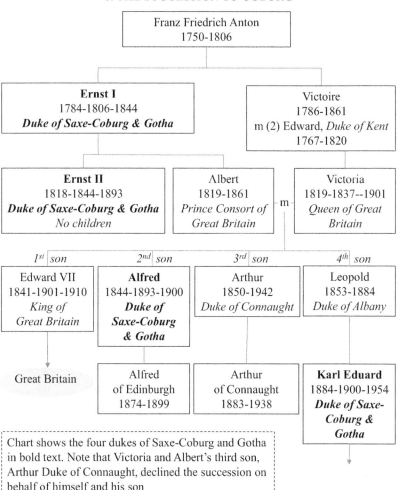

Franz Friedrich Anton
1750-1806

Ernst I
1784-1806-1844
Duke of Saxe-Coburg & Gotha

Victoire
1786-1861
m (2) Edward, *Duke of Kent*
1767-1820

Ernst II
1818-1844-1893
Duke of Saxe-Coburg & Gotha
No children

Albert
1819-1861
Prince Consort of
Great Britain

m

Victoria
1819-1837--1901
Queen of Great
Britain

1st son

Edward VII
1841-1901-1910
King of
Great Britain

2nd son

Alfred
1844-1893-1900
Duke of
Saxe-Coburg
& Gotha

3rd son

Arthur
1850-1942
Duke of Connaught

4th son

Leopold
1853-1884
Duke of Albany

Great Britain

Alfred
of Edinburgh
1874-1899

Arthur
of Connaught
1883-1938

Karl Eduard
1884-1900-1954
Duke of Saxe-
Coburg &
Gotha

Chart shows the four dukes of Saxe-Coburg and Gotha
in bold text. Note that Victoria and Albert's third son,
Arthur Duke of Connaught, declined the succession on
behalf of himself and his son

7. THE THRONES DESCENDED FROM QUEEN VICTORIA

Queen Victoria

Vicky	Wilhelm II		*Prussia/Germany*
	Sophie m *Constantine I*		*Greece*
Bertie	George VI		*Great Britain*
	Maud m *Haakon VII*		*Norway*
Alice	Alix m *Nicholas II*		*Russia*
Affie	Marie m *Ferdinand*		*Romania*
Arthur	Margaret m *Gustaf VI Adolf*		*Sweden*
Beatrice	Victoria Eugenie m *Alfonso XIII*		*Spain*

Chart shows selected children and grandchildren of Queen Victoria.
Her eldest daughter (Vicky) became empress of Germany; her eldest son (Bertie)
king of Great Britain. Five of her granddaughters became queens;
a sixth (Margaret) died before her husband became king of Sweden but her
descendants still sit on that throne.

LIST OF ILLUSTRATIONS

1. Victoria as a new widow in a mournful portrait next to Albert's bust (engraving by William Holl after Albert Graefle, published 1864).
2. Victoria gazes devotedly at Albert in this life-sized statue of the couple in period costume (statue by William Theed now on display in the National Portrait Gallery).
3. Victoria in her widow's cap after a quarter of a century as a widow (cartes-de-visite photograph of 1887 by Lafayette of Dublin).
4. Four generations of British monarchs photographed in 1894 (photo by Percy Lewis Pocock for W. & D. Downey, London, 16 July 1894, at the christening of the future duke of Windsor).
5. Victoria in the last year of her life (print published on 30 March 1900).
6. Albert's mausoleum at Frogmore; Victoria chose the site within days of his death and often visited during her widowhood (published around 1900).
7. Statue of Albert at Balmoral (erected by Victoria in 1867, this statue shows Albert with his much-loved greyhound, called Eos).
8. As a widow Victoria spent as little time as possible at Buckingham Palace (the Garden Front of Buckingham Palace in London, the queen's official residence, published in 1897).
9. In this photo with Bertie and his new bride on their wedding day, Victoria defies the joy of the occasion and gazes grimly at Albert's bust (from a photo by Mayall, 1863).
10. Bertie, the affable prince of Wales, and his beautiful young Danish wife Alexandra (Alix); they were very popular and perversely Victoria was jealous (HRH The Prince of Wales 1863, from a picture by Henry Weigall: Queen Alexandra by John Alfred Vintner, lithograph published 1863).
11. Alix with her first child, Albert Victor (Their Royal Highnesses the Princess of Wales and Albert Victor of Wales, engraving by William Holt Jr after a photograph by Vernon Heath, published 1864).
12. Bertie with his two sons, Albert Victor (Eddy) and George (Georgie) at the time they became naval cadets (HRH The Prince of Wales and his sailor sons; colour print from The Boy's Own Paper. The princes became naval cadets in 1877).
13. Victoria and Bertie in the carriage procession to St Paul's for the Thanksgiving Service for his recovery from typhoid (from the picture by N. Chevalier).
14. Victoria in 1875 – she was gradually recovering from Albert's death (HM Queen Victoria 1875 from a picture by Heinrich Von Angeli).
15. Victoria liked fresh air and hated hot rooms and closed windows – here she

takes afternoon tea out-of-doors, sitting in her carriage.

16. John Brown was a burly highlander (from a photograph by G. W. Wilson, Aberdeen).

17. Balmoral Castle in the Scottish highlands (photograph published in 1887).

18. Landseer's 1867 portrait of the queen with John Brown drew unwelcome attention to her Highland Servant (Queen Victoria at Osborne from the painting by Sir Edwin Landseer).

19. John Brown in attendance (left, wearing a kilt) as Victoria presents a military medal (newspaper cutting, probably from the second half of the 1870s). Also in the picture are the duke and duchess of Edinburgh (Affie and Marie are behind Victoria) and Beatrice (to her mother's left). The recipient of the medal is Commander Purvis.

20. Victoria in a photo of 1866 (carte-de-visite photograph by Disdéri).

21. Victoria with Disraeli when she visited his home at Hughenden Manor (from the woodcut by J. Durand; they are shown at the railway station at the end of the visit).

22. This colourful print commemorates Bertie's tour of India in 1876 (1876 Commemoration of the visit of HRH The Prince of Wales to India; Lithograph Armitage and Ibbotson, Bradford, Yorkshire).

23. Victoria's second daughter, Alice, in a portrait before her father died (lithograph by Richard James Lane after Franz Xaver Winterhalter, 1859).

24. Victoria's third and fourth daughters – Helena (Lenchen) on the right and Louise on the left (Her Royal Highness Princess Helena, lithograph by Léon Noel after Franz Xaver Winterhalter; Her Royal Highness Princess Louise, lithograph by J.A Vintner after Franz Xaver Winterhalter).

25. Victoria with *Baby* (her youngest daughter Beatrice) and their dogs (HM Queen Victoria and HRH the Princess Beatrice, from a photograph probably taken at Osborne around 1875).

26. Caricature of Beatrice at the time of her marriage (Figaro Cartoon by J. Austin).

27. Beatrice married Henry of Battenberg in the village church at Whippingham on the Isle of Wight on 23 July 1885.

28. Victoria commissioned this group portrait of fifty-four of her family members (The Royal family on the Occasion of Queen Victoria's Jubilee, from the picture by Laurits Tuxen, 1887).

29. A caricature portrait of Eddy ('Eddie' by Hay, lithograph by Vincent Brooks, Day and Son, published by Vanity Fair, October 13 1888).

30. Queen Victoria at the time of her Golden Jubilee (Souvenir Portrait of Her Most Gracious Majesty Queen Victoria Empress of India; photograph by Walery transferred onto silk and coloured, 1887).

NOTES

1. Elizabeth Longford, *Victoria RI*, 301.
2. Roger Fulford (edited), *Dearest Mama*, 23. Letter from Victoria (at Windsor Castle) to her eldest daughter, Vicky (in Berlin), 18 December 1861.
3. Queen Victoria's journal. RA VIC/MAIN/QVJ(W) Saturday 7 December 1861 (Princess Beatrice's copies), retrieved 5 August 2017.
4. Arthur Benson and Viscount Esher (edited), *The Letters of Queen Victoria: 1837-1861*, Volume III 605-606. Letter from Victoria (at Osborne House) to King Leopold, 24 December, 1861.
5. George Earl Buckle (edited), *The Letters of Queen Victoria: 1862-1878*, Volume 1 295-296. Letter from Victoria (at Osborne House) to Prime Minister Earl Russell, 22 January 1866.
6. Elizabeth Longford, *Victoria RI*, 313.
7. The alleged comment was referred to in Disraeli's memoirs and is mentioned in Daisy Hay, *Mr and Mrs Disraeli: A Strange Romance* (London: Vintage, 2015), 206.
8. Kate Hubbard. *Serving Victoria: Life in the Royal Household*, 1. Georgiana Liddell was appointed a maid-of-honour in 1841.
9. Christopher Hibbert, *Queen Victoria in Her Letters and Journals*, 179. Letter from Victoria to King Leopold, 12 November 1863.
10. Roger Fulford (edited), *Your Dear Letter*, 22. Letter from Victoria (at Windsor Castle) to Vicky (in Berlin), 5 April 1865.
11. George Earl Buckle (edited), *The Letters of Queen Victoria: 1862-1878*, Volume 1 449. Letter from Victoria to Lord Charles Fitzroy (a member of the royal household), 20 July 1867.
12. Michaela Reid, *Ask Sir James*, 55. Victoria was writing to John Brown's sister-in-law (the wife of his brother Hugh).
13. Christopher Hibbert, *Disraeli: A Personal History*, 402.
14. Roger Fulford (edited), *Dearest Mama*, 85. Letter from Victoria to Vicky, 2 July 1862 (the day after Alice's wedding).
15. Roger Fulford (edited), *Your Dear Letter*, 42. Letter from Victoria to Vicky, 11 September 1865.
16. George Earl Buckle (edited), *The Letters of Queen Victoria: 1862-1878*, Volume 1, 633. Letter from Victoria to Bertie, 29 November 1869.
17. Roger Fulford (edited), *Your Dear Letter*, 200. Letter from Victoria to Vicky, 10 July 1868.
18. Victoria's will of 25 October 1897, held in the Royal Archives. Quoted in Elizabeth Longford, *Victoria RI*, 233-4.

19. Queen Victoria's journal. RA VIC/MAIN/QVJ(W) Tuesday 1 January 1901 (Princess Beatrice's copies), retrieved 3 December 2016.

20. Michaela Reid, *Ask Sir James*, 201.

21. James Pope-Hennessy, *Queen Mary*, 353.

22. Michaela Reid, *Ask Sir James*, 207. From a memo written by Victoria (possibly in 1875), which she handed to Sir James Reid on 12 February 1898.

SELECTED BIBLIOGRAPHY

The list below includes some of my favourite books and also other sources used for *Victoria the Widowed Queen*. They are shown in order by date of publication, starting with the earliest.

G. Barnett Smith, *Life of Her Majesty Queen Victoria*. London: George Routledge and Sons, 1887.

Sir Herbert Maxwell, *Sixty Years a Queen: The Story of Her Majesty's Reign*. London: Harmsworth Bros Ltd, 1897.

Mrs Margaret Oliphant, *The Domestic Life of the Queen*. London: Cassell and Company, 1901.

The Life and Times of Queen Victoria. London: Cassell and Company, 1901.

Arthur Benson and Viscount Esher (edited), *The Letters of Queen Victoria: 1837-1861*. London: John Murray, 1908.

George Earl Buckle (edited), *The Letters of Queen Victoria: 1862-1878*. London: John Murray, 1926.

Arthur Ponsonby, *Henry Ponsonby, Queen Victoria's Private Secretary: His Life from his Letters*. London: Macmillan and Co, 1943.

Helmut and Alison Gernsheim, *Queen Victoria: A Biography in Word and Picture*. London: Longmans, 1959.

John Montgomery, *Royal Dogs: The Pets of British Sovereigns from Victoria to Elizabeth II*. London: Max Parrish, 1962.

Elizabeth Longford, *Victoria RI*. London: Heron Books with Weidenfeld and Nicolson, 1964.

Roger Fulford (edited), *Private Correspondence of Queen Victoria and the Crown Princess of Prussia/German Crown Princess*. London: Evans Brothers, volume covering 1861-1864 published in 1968; 1865-1871 in 1971; 1871-1878 in 1976; 1878-1885 in 1981.

Tom Cullen, *The Empress Brown: The True Story of a Victorian Scandal*. Boston: Houghton Mifflin, 1969.

Barry St-John Nevill (edited), *Life at the Court of Queen Victoria, 1861-1901: Illustrated from the Collection of Lord Edward Pelham-Clinton, Master of the Household*. Exeter: Webb and Bower, 1984.

Christopher Hibbert, *Queen Victoria in her letters and journals: a selection by Christopher Hibbert*. New York: Viking, 1985.

Michaela Reid, *Ask Sir James*. London: Hodder & Stoughton, 1987.

HRH The Duchess of York and Benita Stoney, *Travels with Queen Victoria*. London: Weidenfeld and Nicholson, 1993.

Marlene A. Eilers, *Queen Victoria's Descendants*. Falköping, Sweden: Rosvall

Royal Books, 1997.

Kate Hubbard. *Serving Victoria: Life in the Royal Household*. London: Chatto & Windus, 2012.

Paul Thomas Murphy. *Shooting Victoria: Madness, Mayhem and the Rebirth of the British Monarchy*. London: Head of Zeus, 2012.

Helen Rappaport, *Magnificent Obsession: Victoria, Albert and the Death that Changed the Monarchy*. London: Windmill Books, 2012.

Queen Victoria's Journals: www.queenvictoriasjournals.org. Windsor: The Royal Archives, 2012.

Theo Aronson, *Heart of a Queen: Queen Victoria's Romantic Attachments*. London: Thistle Publishing, 2014.

Annie Gray, *The Greedy Queen: Eating with Victoria*. London: Profile Books, 2017.

Shranbani Basu, *Victoria & Abdul: The Extraordinary Story of The Queen's Closest Confidant*. Stroud: The History Press, 2017.

Queen Victoria has a life story that is full of drama, intrigue, and surprises. She is the British monarch in history whose name everyone knows. Susan Symon's series of books focus on the queen as a woman – her personal life, events that formed her resolute character, and relationships that were important to her. They are illustrated throughout with portraits and memorabilia from the author's collection and use some of Victoria's own words, from her letters and journal, to help tell the story.

If you thought history was dull, this author will make you think again. Roseland Arts Festival.

Young Victoria covers the bizarre events of Victoria's birth, when there was a scramble to produce the next heir to the throne; her lonely childhood under a tough regime; and the national adulation when she came to the throne aged eighteen. *Victoria & Albert* tells the story of one of the most famous relationships in history. There were early troubles with a personality clash and struggle for dominance in the relationship. They came through these to create a true partnership and found a dynasty.

The style is lively and the illustrations gorgeous. I highly recommend this book! Amazon review.

Victoria the Widowed Queen covers the long years of Victoria's widowhood when she became an icon of the age and matriarch of a huge clan. The first years as a widow were the least successful of her reign. She refused to appear in public and her popularity suffered. She gradually emerged from gloom but her seclusion in remote homes fuelled rumours about her private life. Her relationship with a servant caused scandal and later in life she had a puzzling relationship with a young Indian man.

Susan is on a mission to promote royal history to as many readers as possible.
Royalty Digest Quarterly Journal

Victoria's Daughters explores the stories of Queen Victoria's five daughters, tinged with drama, tragedy and scandal. Victoria had qualities that made her a great queen, but she was not at her best as a mother. The princesses were born into privilege and deference. But their lives were blighted by the early death of their father, Prince Albert, and dominated by the demands of their controlling mother. Her daughters were important public figures in their own time but are largely forgotten today.

Susan has done another fantastic job, proving that history can also be fun...
Eurohistory: The European Royal History Journal

QUEEN VICTORIA IN CORNWALL
THE ROYAL VISIT TO CORNWALL IN 1846

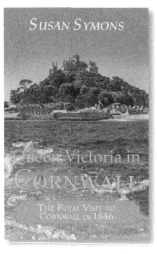

SUSAN SYMONS

On the evening of Friday 4 September 1846, the royal yacht *Victoria and Albert* steamed into the harbour at Falmouth in Cornwall flying the royal standard. On board were Queen Victoria, her husband Prince Albert, and their two eldest children – five-year-old Vicky (Victoria, princess royal) and four-year-old Bertie (Albert Edward, prince of Wales). Their arrival in Falmouth was part of the royal visit to Cornwall when Victoria came ashore to see the sights, meet the local aristocracy in their great houses, and patronise local industries.

Queen Victoria in Cornwall follows in Victoria's footsteps to revisit the sights she saw. There was huge public interest in Victoria's young son. As the eldest son of the sovereign Bertie was the duke of Cornwall from birth and the first duke to visit Cornwall for two hundred years.

With colour illustrations, sketch maps, and family trees, the book should appeal to anyone who enjoys history, or follows royalty, or likes sightseeing in Cornwall.

Cover image:
St Michael's Mount, Cornwall
(Miraphoto/Shutterstock)

THE SCHLOSS SERIES OF BOOKS

Schloss is the German word for castle or palace and you are never far from one of these in Germany. For most of its history Germany was not a single country but a patchwork of royal states, held together under the banner of the Holy Roman Empire. The dukes and princes who ruled these states were passionate builders. Their beautiful castles and palaces, and their compelling personal stories, provide the material for the Schloss series of books.

Each of the Schloss books includes twenty-five beautiful castles and palaces in Germany and looks at these from two aspects. The first is the author's experience as a visitor; the second, colourful stories of the historical royal families that built and lived in them.

Royalty were always the celebrities of there day and their stories from history can rival anything in Hello magazine. The Schloss books might encourage you to go and see these wonderful castles and palaces for yourself.

This book can be seen as an inspiration ... to get there and find the lesser known palaces and learn more about their history.
Royalty Digest Quarterly Journal.

Printed in Great Britain
by Amazon

36734641R00056